KT-174-370

Dravograd

Slovenj Gradec

MARIBOR

Murska Sobota

Lendava

Ptuj

Drava

Slovenska

Slov. Konjice

Velenje

Rogaška Slatina

Celje

Sentjur p.C.

Trbovlje

Hrastnik

Radece

Sevnica

Krško

Trebnje

Brežice

ZAGREB

Novo Mesto

Kočevje Crnomelj

Karlovac

0 - 200 m

200 - 1000 m

500 - 1000 m

1000 - 1500 m

1500 - 2000 m

—— main road

—— secondary road

0   25 km

0   25 miles

New EU Countries and Citizens

Slovenia

Danica Večerić

A Cherrytree Book

This edition published in 2006 by Evans Brothers Limited
2A Portman Mansions
Chiltern Street
London W1U 6NR, UK

Reprinted 2006
Published by arrangement with KIT Publishers, The Netherlands

British Library Cataloguing-in-Publication Data
Veceric, Danica
Slovenia. - (New EU countries and citizens)
1. Slovenia - Juvenile literature
I. Title
943.7'3
ISBN 1842343270
9781842343272

Text: © Danica Veceric 2004
Photographs: Jan Willem Bultje
Translation: Howard Turner
UK editing: Sonya Newland
Design and Layout: Grafisch Ontwerpbureau Agaatsz BNO, Meppel, The Netherlands
Cover: Big Blu Ltd
Cartography: Armand Haye, Amsterdam, The Netherlands
Production: J & P Far East Productions, Soest, The Netherlands

Picture Credits

Photographs: Slovenian Tourist Board, Ljubljana, Slovenia
p. 5 (b), 13 (b), 15 (t),13 (c), 26, 34, 35, 29, 30 (t), 39 (b):Jan Willem Bultje;
p. 11(t) © Hulton-Deutsch Collection/CORBIS; p. 47(t) © SRDJAN ZIVULOVIC/
Reuters/CORBIS; p. 47(b) © Nikola Solic/Reuters/CORBIS

Contents

Introduction

Slovenia lies to the south of Central Europe, on the Adriatic coast between Austria, Hungary, Croatia and Italy. Slovenes sometimes refer to it as the 'country on the sunny side of the Alps' because although large parts of it are mountainous, the south-western coastline enjoys a warm Mediterranean climate.

Although it only became a country in its own right at the end of the twentieth century, Slovene people have lived on this territory continuously since the sixth century. The various political events and territorial aspirations of their stronger neighbours have caused the country's frontiers to change, and as a result many Slovene communities have been isolated outside its borders in Austria, Italy and Hungary.

Slovenia lies at the crossroads of four very different European regions, and its landscape and climate vary greatly across the country. It has mountains, lowlands, rolling hills and beaches. It also has a vast and dramatic karst landscape, in which the limestone rock has been worn away to result in thousands of landscape features and formations. Among these are underground rivers and lakes, and many caves – some of them hundreds of metres deep.

Slovenia is one of the youngest European states. Throughout history the Slovenian territories have been annexed to other countries. Slovenia was made part of Yugoslavia after the Second World War, and remained so until it was granted independence in 1991.

Slovenia has one of the most stable economies of all the countries that were part of the former Yugoslavia. Others have been affected by war and conflict, but Slovenia has remained peaceful. Since its independence, the country has become a member of several important international organisations, working towards peace, security, economic development, and aid for people in need all over the world. It was accepted as a full member of the United Nations a year after its independence. The country is also a member of NATO and the European Council. It joined the European Union on 1 May 2004.

Tourism has increased a lot since the country gained independence, as more and more people discovered the mountains, which are ideal for skiing, and the Mediterranean climate on the small strip of coastline on the Adriatic Sea. It may be small, but Slovenia is one of the most varied and interesting countries in Europe.

▲ The Opera House in Slovenia's capital Ljubljana.

▼ Many villages in Slovenia are built on hilltops. This is the village of Štanjel.

History

The Slovenes are descendants of the Slavic tribes that migrated to the eastern Alps in the second half of the sixth century AD. By the end of the seventh century AD they occupied the area that is now Slovenia as well as territories throughout the Alps, all the way to the River Danube and what is now Vienna.

▼ *Predjama Castle is built into the rock. The present building dates from the sixteenth century, but there has been a fortress here since 1201.*

The Slovenes banished most of the existing settlers, including the Celts, and became neighbours to the Bavarians, Longobards, Avars and Byzantines, with whom they often fought. The 'state' that the Slovenes established on this territory was called Karantania. The centre of Karantania was located at Karnburg, close to what is now Klagenfurt in southern Austria. The state was governed by a duke, who was installed following a special ceremony, at which he had to swear to be a fair and judicious ruler, and to ensure the well-being of his people and lands.

Martin Krpan

Martin Krpan is a Slovenian folk hero. He made his living by smuggling salt – a very costly item – from the coast of what is now Austria to his village in Slovenia. He had a reputation for great strength and, although his smuggling activities were illegal, the Austrian emperor called upon Martin to help defeat the Turkish giant Brdavs, who had killed many men, including the emperor's son. Martin succeeded in killing this man, whom so many feared. The emperor was grateful and offered Martin great riches and even his daughter's hand in marriage, but the empress would not agree to this. Martin was angry at her ingratitude, and said he would never come to Vienna's aid again. Instead he was granted a license to legally transport salt to Slovenia.

▲ *Martin Krpan fighting Brdavs.*

In the eighth century, Christianity began to spread across the region. The Karantanians learned about it from their neighbours and eventually adopted the religion themselves. The spread of Christianity helped in the development of the written word, and this led to the creation of the Freising manuscripts in the tenth century. These are the oldest-known written records in the Slovenian language.

Germanic rule

In AD 748, the Karantanians lost their independence to their stronger Germanic neighbours, who became their overlords. During the time of Germanic rule, the German language was widely used, and the Slovenian language was only preserved amongst the peasant population.

▲ *Otočec Castle stands on an islet in the Krka River, in southern Slovenia. It dates from the thirteenth century.*

In the ninth century, new enemies appeared on the borders of Karantania – the Hungarians. To make it easier to defend the territory, Karantania was divided into several smaller regions. Five main territories emerged, and remained as separate regions until 1918: Styria, Carinthia, Carniola, Gorivka and Primorska. These regions were occupied by Slovenes and Germanic peoples.

By the Middle Ages Slovenian territories were ruled by important feudal families such as the Spanheims, Babensburgs and, in the fourteenth century, the powerful Habsburg family. For a few decades the Celje dukes took over the territories, but when the last Duke of Celje, Ulrik II, died in 1456, most of the Slovenian lands fell completely under Habsburg rule.

Turkish attacks

In the second half of the fifteenth century Turks began raiding Slovenia. They pillaged and plundered, and many of the inhabitants were either killed or taken into slavery. Small boys were carried off to Turkey to be raised as janissaries – the cruellest of Turkish soldiers.

At first the Turks only plundered Slovenia, but by the middle of the fifteenth century the raids had turned into an attempted invasion. They were stopped by the Hungarian king, Matija Korvin. The Slovene people remember him in folksongs and legends as King Matjaž.

▲ *A likeness of Primož Trubar, who helped spread the Slovenian language through his books.*

Protestantism

In the sixteenth century a new religious movement spread from the surrounding countries. Protestantism – literally a movement that 'protested' against the corruption of the Catholic Church – was sweeping through Europe.

In Slovenia the leader of the Protestant movement was Primož Trubar, who wrote the first true Slovenian books – a catechism (a book about the principles of Christianity) and a spelling-book. Trubar also encouraged other writers and this resulted in more books in the Slovenian language. Jurij Dalmatin translated the Bible into Slovenian and Hieronim Megiser compiled the first multi-language dictionary, bringing the Slovenian language to the attention of other European nations. During this period the first printing-house was established in the capital, Ljubljana.

▼ *The old town centre of Piran, with a statue of the composer Giuseppe Tartini, who was born here in 1692.*

The golden age

From the sixteenth century onwards Slovenia began to develop economically. Factories were built, the rivers were busy with traffic and a transport system was established. During the eighteenth century, many reforms were introduced by Empress Maria Theresa, wife of the Holy Roman Emperor, and life in the region began to improve for the peasant population. In particular, the empress insisted that all children should go to school. This was a golden period for Slovenia. Poets and authors started writing in the Slovenian language and the people began to be more aware of their history and culture.

The French emperor Napoleon wanted to reduce the power of the Habsburgs, and in 1809 he seized what he called the Illyrian Provinces, which included present-day Slovenia. Napoleon allowed the Slovenes to use their own language in schools and workplaces. Even after the French gave up control of the lands, many of the reforms they had put in place in education, law and administration, were maintained.

▲ *Empress Maria Theresa.*

The Illyrian Provinces were returned to the Habsburgs in 1814 and remained under their rule for the next century.

Until 1848, the Slovenes did not use the name Slovenia for their country. Instead they called themselves Carniolans, Styrians or Carinthians according to area from which they came. The rulers of the Slovenian territories were Germans, Hungarians and Italians. The official language was German, and Slovenian was only spoken in the countryside.

In 1848, revolution swept across Europe, including Slovenia. There was demand for social and political reform. In Vienna, Slovene intellectuals wrote the first political programme, entitled *Unified Slovenia*. In this programme they demanded that the Slovenian language receive equal status to German, and that Carniola, Carinthia, Styria and a fourth region called Primorska should unify under the name Slovenia.

▶ *The former monastery of Kostanjevica, founded in the seventeenth century.*

▲ *Mementoes of the First World War can be found in the museum at Kobarid in western Slovenia.*

The First World War

At the beginning of the First World War (1914–18) Slovenia was still part of the Austro-Hungarian Empire. Young Slovenian men were drafted into the Austrian army. One of the European front lines during the war was the Soča front, alongside the River Soča in the Alps. Here, fighting took place between the Austrians and the Italians. A great number of young Slovenian soldiers lost their lives in this campaign. The civilian inhabitants of the region suffered starvation and many died from disease; thousands more were forced to flee as the battles raged.

During the war some political parties called for the southern Slav nations to join together under one flag. In 1918, following the disintegration of the Austro-Hungarian Empire, the Slovenes, Croats and Serbs declared themselves an independent country on 1 December 1918. They called this the Kingdom of Serbs, Croats and Slovenes. In 1929 this country was renamed the Kingdom of Yugoslavia.

◀ *The Soča River in the Alps, on the border between Slovenia and Italy, was the front line in this region during the First World War.*

The Second World War

In the first months of the Second World War (1939–45), the Kingdom of Yugoslavia remained relatively unaffected by the fighting going on elsewhere in Europe. However, on 6 April 1941, the area was attacked by armies of Germans, Italians and Hungarians. They wreaked havoc – burning down villages and sending inhabitants to concentration camps. By the time the war ended, much of the country's infrastructure had been destroyed and its population displaced. The Slovenes, Croats, Serbs, Montenegrins and Macedonians created a new country called the Federal Republic of Yugoslavia. They elected Joseph Tito as their president. At first Tito's policies were very much in line with those of the communist Soviet Union; however he soon began to move away from this, and Yugoslavia split with the Soviet Union in 1948. Tito strongly disapproved of the Russian invasions of Hungary in 1956 and Czechoslovakia in 1968.

After Tito's death in May 1980, no one could decide how to run a country that was inhabited by so many different nations. The republic continued for another 10 years, but several of the regions wanted to become independent states. Slovenia declared independence on 25 June 1991. In response, Yugoslavia mobilised its army, but pressure from the European Union ensured that the battle lasted only 10 days. Slovenia had won its independence. In May 1992 the country was admitted to the United Nations, and this has been followed by membership of several other international organisations, including the European Union, on 1 May 2004.

▲ German soldiers in a Slovenian village on the Drava River, in 1941.

Joseph Tito

Tito was born on 25 May 1892 to a peasant family in the village of Kumrovec, in present-day Croatia. During the First World War he fought in the Austrian (Habsburg) army, and was taken prisoner and sent to Russia. There he witnessed the overthrow of the Russian tsar and the introduction of the communist government. In 1920, Tito returned to Zagreb – now in the new Kingdom of Serbs, Croats and Slovenes – and in 1928 he became secretary of the Communist Party, which was forbidden at that time. He was arrested and spent five years in prison. He was not put off, however, and in 1937 he began to reorganise the Communist Party. Throughout the Second World War, Tito led the resistance against the German and Italian occupiers. During this period, the Communist Party became the most powerful political group in the region and at the end of the war Tito became president of the Federal Republic of Yugoslavia.

▼ Joseph Tito, the first president of the Federal Republic of Yugoslavia.

The country

Slovenia is one of the smaller countries in Europe, both in terms of size and population. It covers an area of 20,273 km² and it has a population of just over two million. It has dramatic mountains and fertile lowlands, tranquil lakeland and bustling cities, inland rivers and sunny beaches.

The countryside in Slovenia is diverse. Four European landscapes meet in this region – the Alps, the Pannonian Lowlands, the Dinar mountain range and the Mediterranean.

Three Alpine ranges occupy the north-western part of Slovenia – the Julian Alps, the Kamniško-Savinjske Alps and the Karavanken Mountains. The highest peak is Triglav (2,864 metres). As well as the snow-covered peaks, there are several lakes in this region, including Lake Bled, Lake Bohinj and the seven Triglav lakes. Numerous rivers flow down from the Alps, forming rapids, waterfalls and narrow gorges.

▼ *Lake Bled, in Slovenia's Alpine region, is renowned for its beauty.*

The Pannonian Lowlands continue from Slovenia into Hungary and Croatia. Here, numerous hills interchange with valleys and plains. The hills are covered with forests and are ideal for the cultivation of vines and fruit trees. Wheat, corn, sugar beet and potatoes are grown in the fertile fields.

The Dinar mountain range starts in the southern part of Slovenia and continues along the Adriatic coast. The landscape is composed of limestone and both on the surface and below the ground are karst features such as underground caves, lakes and sinkholes. The karst tablelands are covered with woods, many of which are beautifully preserved, particularly those in Kočevski Rog.

Slovenia is a coastal country. It lies on the Adriatic coast, which is a part of the larger Mediterranean Sea. The coast offers the people of Slovenia a 'window on the world', because ships from many other countries can reach the port of Koper here. The warmth of the Adriatic coast makes it popular with tourists during the summer months, when the sea temperature can reach a pleasant 27°C. In the winter it cools to 12°C. The sea is also an important source of salt, which is harvested via salt-pans. In the Bay of Trieste the Adriatic Sea reaches its northernmost point. The coastal territories have a warm climate and evergreen vegetation.

▲ *The Triglav lakes lie in the national park of the same name. Each of the seven lakes has a different mineral composition and therefore a different colour.*

▲ *The most famous salt-pans are the ones at Sečovlje.*

◄ *The Pannonian Lowlands consist of flat plains, valleys and tree-covered hills.*

Rivers

Slovenia is a land of water. The best-known rivers are the Sava, Drava and Soča. The poet Simon Gregorčič wrote about the Soča: 'You are beautiful, the clear daughter of the mountains, graceful in your natural beauty....'

The river Drava rises in neighbouring Austria. Because the water in the river is plentiful throughout the year, it is used by hydroelectric power stations.

The Sava is the longest river in Slovenia. It continues its course into Croatia and then flows into the River Danube.

In the past, all three of these rivers were used for transporting goods, including timber, coal and wheat, to various cities within Slovenia.

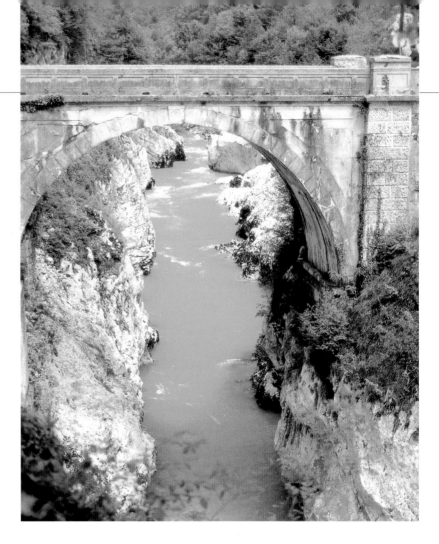

▼ *The Drava River near Ptuj, in the north-east of the country.*

▲ *The Soča River is regarded as the most beautiful river in Slovenia because of the clear blue-green of its water.*

There are several other rivers in Slovenia, which are just as important. The Ljubljanica River runs through the capital Ljubljana; it is also known as 'the river of seven names', because it is known by different names at certain points along its course, including where it runs underground.

Most rivers that alternate between running above the surface and then disappearing underground are found in limestone (karst) landscapes. In such areas the intermittent rivers have dissolved the limestone under the ground and have created impressive underground caves. There are many landscape features like this in Slovenia.

Numerous rivers and streams have formed narrow valleys, gorges and river beds, which can reach 70 metres in depth. The most dramatic gorges can be found on the rivers Radovna, Koritnica, Tolminka and Soča. Waterfalls are also important tourist spots. The most picturesque waterfalls are Savica at Bohinj Lake, Peričnik in the Vrata Valley, Boka on the Soča River and Rinka in the Savinjske Alps.

▶ *These caves near Škocjan have been formed by the river water wearing away the surrounding limestone.*

▲ *The Ljubljanica as it runs through the capital city Ljubljana.*

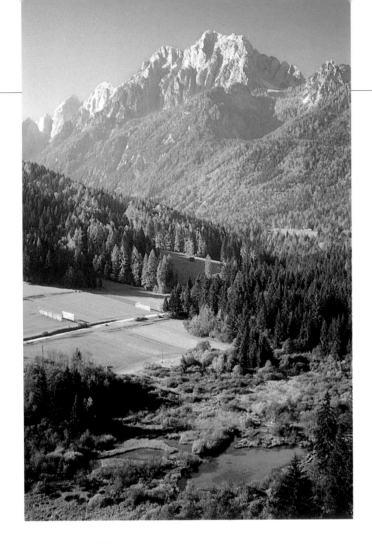

◄ A mountain-pass in the Julian Alps connects the towns of Rateč and Podkoren.

Lakes

Slovenia has numerous lakes of different origins. In the Alps there are glacial lakes, which are the remains of great glaciers that covered the mountain region during the Ice Age. Lakes Bhinj and Bled have glacial origins and both usually freeze during the winter. In the summer, however, they are warm enough to swim in.

The Cerknica Lake is fascinating place to visit. From the autumn to spring it holds water, but in the summer, when there is not enough rainfall to maintain the water levels, the lake empties. The water runs through large sinkholes in the limestone and leaves the bottom of the lake covered with grass.

The water in the Wild Lake near Idrija comes from a karst spring, which flows on into deep caves. There are also several ox-bow lakes, which emerge on river bends. The most famous ones can be found on the River Mura, and many birds make their homes here.

▼ Lake Bohinj.

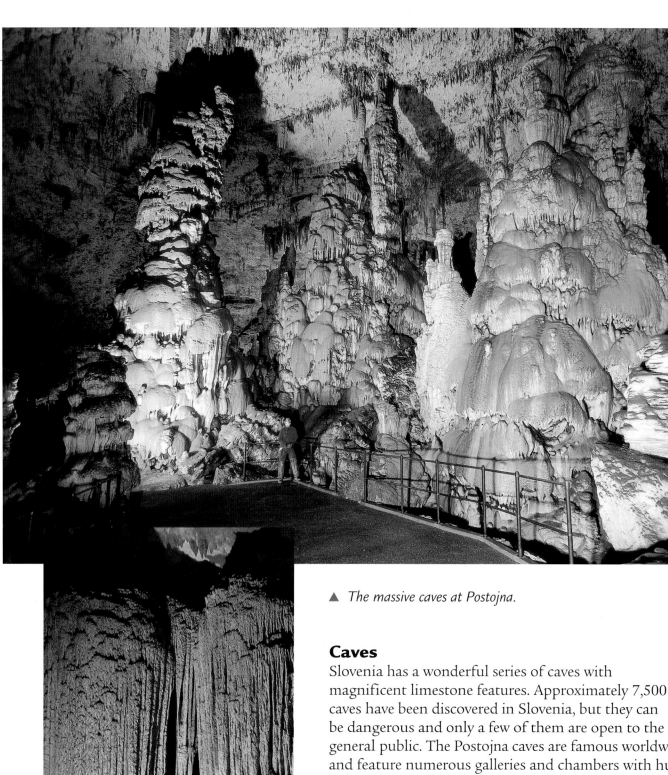

▲ The massive caves at Postojna.

Caves

Slovenia has a wonderful series of caves with magnificent limestone features. Approximately 7,500 caves have been discovered in Slovenia, but they can be dangerous and only a few of them are open to the general public. The Postojna caves are famous worldwide and feature numerous galleries and chambers with huge stalactites. The Škocjan caves, which have underground canyons up to 90 metres high, are now protected by the organisation UNESCO. The Križna cave is renowned for its underground lakes. Numerous animal species have made their home in the caves, ranging from bats and crabs to spiders and the cave salamander (*Proteus anguinus*), a species of amphibian.

◀ Stalactites grow very slowly – on average only a few millimetres every century.

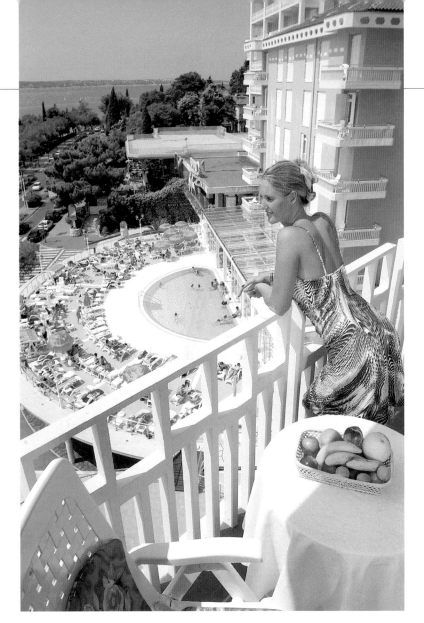

Climate

Like the landscape, Slovenia's climate is diverse. In the mountainous regions the climate is cold and is often referred to as an 'Alpine climate'. The winters are long, cold and snowy. However, this part of the country is ideal for skiing, and there are wonderful slopes on Pohorje, in the vicinity of Kranjska Gora, on Kanin and Krvavec. Summers in the mountains can be pleasantly warm – ideal for hikers who want to explore the mountain peaks. In the summer, the water in the lakes also gets agreeably warm, and visitors can swim here in the natural environment.

Along the Adriatic coast the climate in the summer is hot, and there is not much rainfall. Winters are short and fairly mild. The temperature rarely reaches freezing. Because the Adriatic Sea – which is a part of the Mediterranean Sea – has a great influence upon the climate, this climate is known as 'Mediterranean'. From the karst tablelands strong winds blow towards the sea, and have been known to reach speeds of up to 200 kph.

▲ *Summertime on the Adriatic coast is hot and sunny.*

The rest of Slovenia has a continental climate. Here the summers are long and hot and the winters long and cold. Due to global warming Slovenia has less snow during the winter than it had even in the fairly recent past. There is also less rainfall and therefore the landscape can be affected by drought, especially during the summer months.

▶ *Lake Bled in the winter.*

Towns and cities

In comparison to other European towns and cities, those in Slovenia are quite small. Only 15 of them have more than 10,000 inhabitants. However, the towns are not full of high-rise blocks and they have plenty of parks and gardens. Generally Slovenian towns are pleasant places to live or visit.

▲ *An aerial view of the Slovenian capital Ljubljana.*

The reason that Slovenian towns are so small is that many people still prefer to live in the countryside. Here they can have their own houses rather than flats or apartments, and they can own more land. Farming villages are still common in certain areas of Slovenia. There are even a few farms situated high up in the Alps. There are very few traditional farmhouses left nowadays – most of them have been replaced by modern houses, which offer greater comfort. Some old houses have been turned into museums, which show how people lived in the past. Among the particular architectural curiosities in the country are the Slovenian haysheds, where people would store hay once it had been harvested. Painted beehives are also an interesting feature of the countryside.

Industry and other activities are concentrated in the towns, and workers usually commute daily to the towns from the smaller settlements that have been established in the surrounding areas.

◀ *A traditional hayshed in the Slovenian countryside.*

Ljubljana

Ljubljana is the capital of Slovenia and is its cultural, political and economic centre. This is where the president, the parliament, the constitutional and supreme courts, and most embassies are located. In addition to its primary and secondary schools, Ljubljana has a university. The UNESCO International Centre for Chemical Studies is also based in Ljubljana. The centre of cultural activities can be found in the complex of halls and exhibition pavilions in Cankarjev Dom. Theatres, opera, orchestral halls and museums, as well as the national and university libraries, are all located in the centre of the city.

A great many tourists visit Ljubljana because of its cultural and historic places of interest, for sport, and trade fairs.

▼ *Many brightly coloured houses face the River Ljubljanica in the capital.*

▶ *The dragon is the symbol of Ljubljana. The inhabitants of the city are nicknamed 'zmajceki', which means 'little dragons'.*

◀ The Preator Palace in Koper was the head-quarters of the Venetian government when the town was a part of the Venetian Republic.

Koper

Koper is a coastal town situated on the Gulf of Trieste. It is Slovenia's major fishing port and is also a centre for salt mining. The town spent more than 500 years under the rule of the Venetians, and when the Republic of Venice was dissolved, ownership of the town passed to Austria and then Italy, before becoming part of Yugoslavia and subsequently Slovenia.

Ptuj

Ptuj, in north-eastern Slovenia is the oldest town in the country, and dates from Roman times, although much of the present look and feel of the town dates from the Middle Ages, when it experienced a rise in wealth and prosperity. There are plenty of museums and galleries in Ptuj, as well as the fascinating archeological remains from ancient times. Roman remains can also be found in Ljubljana, Celje, and Ajdovščina.

Škofja Loka

One of the best-preserved medieval towns in Slovenia is Škofja Loka, which was founded by the bishops of Freiburg in AD 973. In the fourteenth century a town wall was built, with five entrance gates, each one guarded by a watchtower. Much of the wall remains today. The town also has a castle and several old churches.

Maribor

Maribor is another town with a long history – people were living here on the banks of the Drava River as early as the twelfth century. Although it is now an important industrial centre, with a number of factories, there are several historical buildings still standing, including a twelfth-century Gothic cathedral and a fifteenth-century castle.

MESTNA OBČINA

MARIBOR

Dobrodošli Welcome

▶ The city of Maribor on the Drava River.

People and culture

In Slovenia, just over two million people live in an area covering 20,273 km². The population density is lower than in most other European countries and there are, on average, 98 people per km².

The population density is influenced by landscape and climate, both of which are diverse across Slovenia. The number of inhabitants also depends on industrial growth. After the Second World War, large numbers of people moved to the towns and cities from the villages. Population density is also influenced by natural population growth, which has declined in the last few decades because the economic and social climate has been difficult.

Throughout its history Slovenia has experienced several periods when large numbers of people moved away from the region. The largest migrations were caused by difficult economic conditions. Major migrations took place at the end of the nineteenth century and the beginning of the twentieth century. Slovenes mainly migrated to the USA and Australia. After the Second World War a large number of people left to seek temporary work in the more economically developed countries of Germany, Switzerland, Belgium and France. However, many workers from regions such as Serbia, Bosnia Herzegovina and Croatia moved to Slovenia.

Ethnic minorities

Around 88 per cent of the population are Slovene; the rest are minorities. The two main minority groups in Slovenia are Italians, who live in the Koper area, and Hungarians who live in the Prekmurje region. Minorities have the same rights as Slovenes and can freely use their own national symbols and establish schools and other organisations in order to preserve their ethnic identity.

Minorities are are also free to develop their own economic, cultural and scientific research activities. Muslims, Serbs, Albanians, Macedonians, Croats and Montenegrins from what was once Yugoslavia have moved into larger industrial cities in Slovenia. There are also a number of Roma or gypsies in the country, who largely live in the Prekmurje region, the Dolenjska region and in Bela Krajina.

◄ *Locals and tourists wander through the town square in Maribor.*

Language

The official language is Slovenian, a south-Slavic language related to Serbian and Croatian. It is written in the Latin alphabet, but uses many diacritic marks (accents). Hungarian, German and Italian are the tongues spoken by minority groups; these languages are given equal importance with Slovenian.

Religion

The most widespread religion in Slovenia is Roman Catholicism (around 58 per cent of the population), followed by Orthodox Christianity and Muslims (each around 2.4 per cent). The remainder is made up of Protestants and other religions. The Slovenian constitution grants everyone the right to follow their religion of choice. Most of the churches in Slovenia are Roman Catholic, but areas with other religious groups have their own buildings for worship.

Some Slovene words

Good morning	*Dobro jutro*
Please	*Prosim*
Thank you	*Hvala*
Yes	*Da*
No	*Ne*
Good evening	*Dober večer*
Goodbye	*Na svidenje*

1	*ena*
2	*dva*
3	*tri*
4	*štiri*
5	*pet*
6	*šest*
7	*sedem*
8	*osem*
9	*devet*
10	*deset*

State symbols

The main state symbols in Slovenia are the flag, the coat of arms, the national anthem and the country's currency. The Slovenian flag consists of three equal horizontal bands of white, blue and red. The Slovenian seal, a shield with the image of Triglav, Slovenia's highest peak, in white against a blue background is at the centre; beneath it are two wavy blue lines depicting seas and rivers, and above it are three six-pointed stars arranged in an inverted triangle. This symbol is taken from the coat of arms of the Counts of Celje used in the fourteenth and early fifteenth centuries. The seal is located in the upper hoist or mast side of the flag, centred in the white and blue bands.

▲ *Slovenia's national flag.*

◀ *The church of St Francis in Ljubljana.*

▶ *A fragment of the poem* Zdravljica *by France Prešeren, in the poet's own hand. In the nineteenth century, the poem was removed from a volume of Prešeren's poems by the state censor.*

France Prešeren's poem *Zdravljica* was adopted as Slovenia's national anthem in in 1990. It talks of democracy and the people's desire for peace:

> *God's blessing on all nations,*
> *Who long and work for that bright day,*
> *When o'er earth's habitations*
> *No war, no strife shall hold its sway;*
> *Who long to see*
> *That all men free*
> *No more shall foes, but neighbours be.*

The currency in Slovenia is the tolar (SIT). There are around 350 tolars in one British pound, and around 240 in one euro. There are 100 stotins to a tolar.

▲ *Although the official currency is still the Slovenian tolar, the country plans to adopt the euro in 2007.*

France Prešeren

France Prešeren (1800–49) is one of the greatest poets in the history of Slovenia. He was a follower of the Romantic Movement, a period in which emotions found their way into many artistic forms. Prešeren did not have far to look for inspiration: his private life was a rich source. The poet led an unhappy life, he was an alcoholic and forever in love with unattainable women. He died young and penniless from excessive drinking. There are two important recurring themes in Prešeren's work: his desire that his country should be free and his great, unrequited passion for Julija Primic, the daughter of a rich merchant from Ljubljana, who thought Prešeren too lowly for his daughter. His desire for his country's freedom is the subject of his famous poem *Zdravljica* ('The Toast'), which Prešeren wrote in 1844. The poem is an impassioned plea for an independent Slovenia, inspired by the ideals of the French Revolution – freedom, equality and brotherhood. In his poem, Prešeren tried to stress the importance of peaceful relations between the various nations and the right all peoples have to freedom. For Slovenes, France Prešeren is a national hero – the national Day of Culture is held on the anniversary of his death (8 February), and the most prestigious Slovenian Arts Prize is named after him.

Health

Slovenes are health conscious and enjoy many sports – tennis, swimming, cycling and skiing. Alternative therapies and yoga are also popular.

Despite this, Slovenes suffer from the same illnesses and diseases as people in the rest of Europe. Cancer remains the most common disease and there have been a number of cases of HIV and AIDS in the country, although a preventative programme has been set up to restrict its spread. Hospitals can be found in every large city and the capital Ljubljana has several clinics. Health centres take care of the everyday illnesses.

Media

Slovenia has a national television station (TV Slovenia), two commercial television stations and 12 smaller local television stations. International television programmes can be viewed via satellite stations and a wide selection of satellite and cable channels are available. The country also receives programmes from all over the world.

In addition, there is a large number of radio stations, and almost every town has its own local radio. Apart from news and entertainment, radio and television offer educational services.

▲ *This health spa has medicinal springs, which are thought to have therapeutic properties.*

▼ *A television programme being recorded.*

▶ *The market in Ljubljana. Many people buy their fresh fruit, vegetables, cheese and other foods from outdoor markets.*

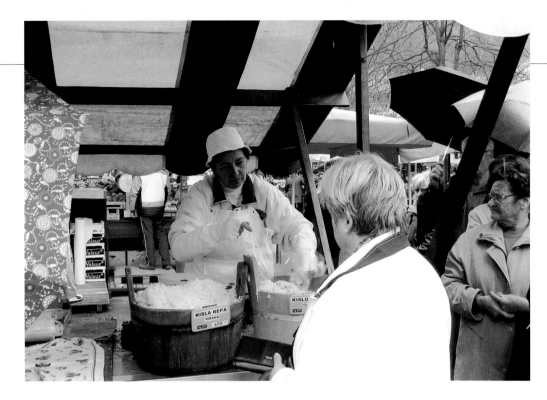

▼ *There are large department stores in the big towns.*

Shopping

Most towns in Slovenia have large shopping centres, with similar shops to other towns and cities in Europe. These shops offer food and commodities from all over the world. Just about every town has a market where people purchase fruit and vegetables, and other fresh produce.

Fast-food restaurants are very popular with young people and most towns have them. There are also many Chinese restaurants, and several others offering cuisine from countries all over the world, such as France, Spain and Mexico.

◀ *A group of singers and dancers from Bela Krajina.*

Entertainment

Young people generally prefer to spend their free time in pubs and clubs. A great number of them attend dance schools, where they learn how to dance Latin American dances, hip-hop and other modern dance styles. Many people visit the cinema to see international films, which quickly find their way to Slovenia. At the weekends various activities are held in the large shopping centres. Many like to visit the theatre, opera and concerts to see and hear local and international singers. On major public holidays numerous parties are organised in towns and villages, which present opportunities for people to dance, have fun and socialise.

▼ *Skiing is a national pastime in Slovenia, and locals and tourists alike enjoy the fine snow on the Alpine slopes.*

◀ *National holidays are causes of colourful celebration in Slovenia. People join their neighbours in the streets, and often fairs and other events are held.*

Festivals

There are a number of festivals and public holidays in Slovenia. There is a Celebration of the Uprising in April, when people remember the day that the country rose against German occupation during the Second World War. Solvenes also celebrate their own independence in December.

Government

Slovenia declared its independence on 25 June 1991. On 23 December the same year the Assembly of the Republic of Slovenia adopted the Constitution of the Republic of Slovenia, which outlined the basis for a new democratic state. All legislation in Slovenia must be in legal agreement with the principles and articles of the constitution. The constitution emphasises the country's belief in universal respect for human rights and basic freedoms for all people.

The government is made up of three major components: the legislature, the executive and the judiciary. The legislature is represented by a parliament with 90 members, which agrees new legislation, and the national council, which offers advice to the parliament.

▲ *A brass band marches through the streets on a public holiday.*

The executive is represented by the government and the president. The government is responsible for making sure that legislation is enforced. This means that the government takes care of education, healthcare, the police force, the armed forces, social security, and many other aspects of everyday life in Slovenia. The president is helped in his duties by his ministers. Judges elect their own leaders.

The president represents the Republic of Slovenia at home and abroad as the head of state and calls elections, presents state awards and also acts as supreme commander of the armed forces. The president is elected directly.

In Slovenia there is also an ombudsman (an office that helps people with complaints) for human rights, which protects the citizens of the Republic of Slovenia in their relations with the state bodies, local authorities and public officials. The ombudsman is elected by parliament after a recommendation made by the president.

▶ *The House of Parliament in Ljubljana.*

Education

Education is compulsory for all children between the ages of six and 15 in Slovenia. Almost all the schools are state-run, and there are only a few private institutions. Schools are funded by the government.

▲ *A school in Ravne na Kasoškem.*

▼ *A sign warns that a school is up ahead and motorists should slow down.*

Elementary school lasts for nine years – the duration of compulsory education in Slovenia. Although the education itself is free, parents have to buy text books and other learning materials.

There must be at least 28 pupils in each class of elementary school, so in less-populated areas classes are often made up of pupils of different ages. In the first four years classes are taught by one teacher, but after this different teachers takes lessons in different subjects.

These boys are walking to school in the rain. They go to elementary school, which lasts nine years. The education system in Slovenia has proved successful. A number of schools have attained the status of a 'healthy school'. This means that they have been recognised for making a special effort to create a caring learning environment. In particular they provide their pupils with healthy meals and teach them to respect the natural environment.

Higher education

At the end of elementary school, pupils take exams and receive a diploma if they pass all their subjects. This diploma allows them to go on to further education in the form of secondary schools – either general or vocational. The marks pupils get in their exams are important – particularly those in maths, Slovenian and a foreign language. At secondary schools children can enrol on either three- or four-year courses in continued general education or in specific subjects that will train them for a profession.

There are more exams at the end of secondary school, after which students can go on to university as undergraduates and later as postgraduates if they want to. There are two universities in Slovenia: Ljubljana University (the largest) and the University of Technology in Maribor.

Slovenia has an efficient education system: there are enough schools to accommodate all children and the facilities are good. Nearly 80 per cent of the adult population has a secondary-school diploma, and around 10 per cent has a university degree. Education is equally available to both sexes.

▶ Students at the University of Technology in Maribor at work on a project.

Cuisine

Slovenian cuisine is as diverse as the country's landscape, and each region has several traditional dishes. Slovenian food is typically very simple but tasty. Most recipes have their origins in rural cooking.

The Slovenes eat a lot of sauerkraut (pickled cabbage) and black pudding. Black pudding is a sausage made of pork and pig's blood, sometimes filled with rice.

Other traditional dishes include boiled buckwheat mash, Idrija *žlikrofi* – potato balls made with herbs and spices, and wrapped in a thin dough. Bread is much-loved by the Slovenes and is served at almost every meal. The best bread is baked in a open-fire oven, and is often made of corn, buckwheat or wheat flour. Nearly every region of Slovenia has its own speciality bread.

Meat

Pork is the most widely eaten meat in Slovenia. Sausages and ham are particular favourites, and there are several regional meat soups. Along the Adriatic coast, legs of pork dried in the open air are a speciality.

◄ Pork meats such as ham and sausages are eaten all over the country.

▲ *Many kinds of fish can be found in the country. Some are cooked to traditional Slovenian recipes, while others are influenced by the cuisine of Slovenia's neighbouring countries.*

Fish

Fish dishes are popular in Slovenia, particularly along the coast. Shellfish and bluefish, which are caught in the Adriatic Sea, are specialities of the region along the coast. Freshwater fish are also abundant in the rivers and lakes in Slovenia and restaurants throughout the country offer a range of delicious fish dishes on their menus.

Slow food

A recent fashion in food in Slovenia is called 'slow food'. A typical meal can take place at a restaurant or at home amongst friends and family. There can be as many as nine courses at a 'slow-food' meal, and these are usually traditional dishes. Everyone takes their time over the meal and often enjoys a different type of wine with each course.

Drink

There are vineyards all across Slovenia, and the tradition of wine-making dates back to Roman times. Because of the country's varied climates – from the Alps to the Mediterranean – many different wines are produced, some of which are gaining a good reputation elsewhere in the world.

▶ *A wine-cellar with large wooden barrels, in which the wine is fermented.*

▼ *Thanks to the mild climate, many kinds of fruit are grown.*

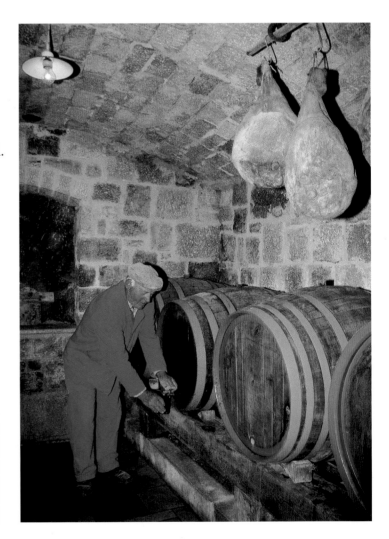

▶ *Potica is a favourite sweet dish in Slovenia.*

Dessert

At large celebrations, desserts are prepared. The most popular are various types of pastries, such as potica. Potica is an old Slovenian dish first mentioned in print in 1689. Potica is baked in round earthenware pots and can be filled with nuts, poppy seeds, cottage cheese, crackling, dried fruit or tarragon.

The oldest of all desserts are the Slovenian honey pastries, which are baked and sold as bread in the shape of hearts. At large-scale celebrations these honey hearts are exchanged by lovers.

Recipe for potica

Ingredients for the dough
1kg white flour, 30g yeast, 3-4 egg yolks, 300ml warm milk, 120g butter or margarine, 1 teaspoon of salt, 2 teaspoons of sugar

Ingredients for the filling
600-700g ground nuts, 200g honey, 50g sugar, 100-200ml milk, 1 egg, cinnamon, a dash of rum

Mix the yeast with a teaspoon of sugar and two tablespoons of flour. Add the salt and 50ml of milk to the mixture and then leave it in a warm place to rise. Sift the rest of the flour into a mixing bowl, make a hole in the centre and add the beaten egg yolks, the rest of the warm milk, and the risen yeast that you mixed earlier. Beat the dough until bubbles appear and it starts to come away from the edge of the bowl easily. Knead it for five minutes, cover it with a clean cloth, and leave it in a warm place to rise.

In the meantime, make the filling. The ground nuts should be scalded with hot milk and the honey should be heated so that it is runny, then added to the nuts. Next, add a bit of cinnamon. Into the slightly cooled filling add one or two eggs. Roll the dough out to form a layer, half a centimetre thick, and cover it evenly with the filling. Roll it tightly and place it on a greased baking tin and let it rise again. Before putting it in the oven, coat it lightly with beaten eggs and then bake it for 70 minutes at 170°C. Cool the baked roll in the mould for at least 15 minutes, then take it out, sprinkle it with sugar and cover it with a napkin to cool completely.

Transport

Due to its geographical position in Europe, Slovenia is criss-crossed by many important transport routes, linking several European countries to the Near East. Even in pre-Roman times numerous nations crossed this territory and mingled and traded with each other.

Slovenia could be considered the place where Eastern and Western Europe meet. Almost everyone travelling from Austria to Croatia or from Italy to Hungary by road passes through the Slovenian capital Ljubljana.

Road and railway transport is increasing across Slovenian territory because of the economic growth of the Eastern European countries that trade with the West across Slovenia. Many motorways are currently under construction to provide a faster and more efficient road-transport system.

Railways

Slovenia has 1,200 km of railway tracks, and all the larger Slovenian cities have railway connections. The first railway was built in 1857 and ran from Vienna, through Ljubljana, to Trieste. Many of the railways are quite old, but the rail system is efficient and trains are one of the most convenient ways of travelling around Slovenia.

Public transport

All the larger cities are connected by bus and rail routes. However, people still prefer to use private cars because this is often the fastest and most comfortable way of travelling around the country. This has resulted in traffic problems around the larger cities and towns, especially those that don't have many car parks.

Pollution is also increasing because of emissions from all the car exhausts. To solve this problem steps are being taken to modernise city and suburban public-transport systems.

▼ The main international airport at Brnik.

Aviation

Brnik Airport is the main international airport in Slovenia. A smaller airport for tourists is located in Portoroz. The national air carrier is Adria Airways, whose routes mainly connect with European cities. Sport aviation in the form of gliding is a popular activity in Slovenia.

Shipping

The largest industrial port is located in Koper. Here, ships dock from all over the world. Cargo is unloaded and transferred to lorries and trains. The port of Koper is also used by Austria, Hungary, the Czech Republic and Slovakia, as they are all landlocked countries without ports of their own.

◀ *The port of Koper.*

▼ *In tourist resorts on the coast there are marinas where it is possible to berth sailing or motor boats. This is the marina in Portoro.*

The economy

Throughout the last century Slovenia's system of economy has been through many changes. Although industry is the most important element of the economy, the country now has good trade relations with many European countries.

Slovenia trades mostly with other countries in the European Union, especially Germany, Italy, Austria and France. However, economic relations with other countries are also improving, both inside and outside the EU. In particular there is greater co-operation with some of the countries that were part of the former Yugoslavia, former Soviet Union countries, and the United States of America.

A growing number of countries are showing an interest in the Slovenian economy. The highest levels of investment has come from Austria, France, Germany and Italy.

▲ *A wine-grower pruning his vines.*

▼ *Cultivating vines and making wine is an important part of the Slovenian economy.*

▲ *The production of semiconductors in the Tovarna plant.*

The largest Slovene exporters

Revoz – production and marketing of cars
Gorenje – production of electric household appliances
Lek – production of pharmaceutical and chemical products
Krka – medicines, production of pharmaceutical products
Prevent – car-seat covers, protective clothing and gloves
Sava Tires – production of tyres for vehicles
Impol – aluminium production
Talum – aluminium production

Industry

Over the last 10 years industry has undergone considerable change in Slovenia. Previously, the metal and textile industries were the most important; in recent years, however, the chemical and car-manufacturing industries have grown stronger and now make important export products. The food-processing industry is successful in the domestic market as well in international trade with countries like Croatia and Bosnia.

The number of employees in the industrial sector has decreased in recent years as more people are employed in trade, tourism and other service activities.

Agriculture

Most farming companies are run as family businesses. Wheat, corn and barley are the main farming products. The farming companies also produce sugar-beet, potatoes, alfalfa, apples and pears in large quantities. Much of the farmland in Slovenia is set aside for vineyards, which are an important part of the agriculture industry.

Much agricultural land is grassland, and cattle-raising is the main farming activity. Farmers produce mainly milk, meat and eggs. Farms are generally quite small, but there are plenty of them across the country.

▲ Lek is a pharmaceutical company that makes medicines.

▼ Pepper-growers in northern Slovenia.

Tourism

Income from tourism is important to the Slovenian economy. Most tourism is focused in the coastal region along the Adriatic, and in the mountains. However, increasing numbers of people are also coming to Slovenia to visit the hot springs in the spa towns.

▼ *White-water rafting on the Alpine Soča River in western Slovenia.*

Slovenia has such a wide variety of landscapes and climates that it is ideal as a holiday destination, and many different activities can be enjoyed. The Slovenian Alps are popular among skiers in the winter, while in the summer there are many hiking trails that offer fantastic views across the region.

▼ *Terme Olimia, with its indoor and outdoor thermal pools, is one of the most popular spa resorts.*

The most challenging peak for mountaineers and climbers is Triglav, the highest mountain in the country. The name Triglav means 'triple head' and was named after a pagan god, revered by the ancient Slovenes. He had three faces – one face that looked back to the past, one that looked into the present and one that looked forward into the future.

▲ A rowing match on Lake Bled in the Julian Alps.

The routes through the mountain regions are some of the most attractive walks in the country, passing through small villages, past lakes and ancient castles, some of which are open to the public. Those in Bled and Ptuj are well known. From the peak of Triglav there are magnificent views of the mountain landscape all around.

It is just a two-hour drive from the Alps to the Adriatic coast. Although Slovenia has only a small strip of coastline, it attracts many holiday-makers. The coast is rocky but the sea is good for swimming, particularly in the summer.

The many caverns in the karst region, the limestone hills in the south-west, are a major tourist attraction. This region features hundreds of crevices, holes, underground rivers and caves, some of which can be explored. The caverns in Postojna are world famous. This is also an important wine-making region.

The use of hot springs for healing purposes dates back to Roman times, and today the spas in Slovenia are becoming increasingly popular with tourists. The most famous spas can be found in Radenci, Terme Olimia and Moravci, as well as Rogaška Slatina – Slovenia's largest and oldest spa town.

◀ Hiking in the mountains in wintertime.

Nature

Slovenia is home to thousands of plant and animal species. The reason for this diversity is the country's location at the junction of four quite different areas in terms of landscape and climate: the Alpine, Mediterranean, Pannonian and the Illyrian-Dinar regions.

Vegetation

More than 50 per cent of Slovene territory is covered by forests. The type of trees found in these forests depends on the climate and height above sea level. In the high mountain regions coniferous forests dominated by pine-trees are typical, but fir-tree forests are very rare. In the coastal region there are many oak forests. In places with a hotter and drier climate there are wild-pine forests. Along the rivers, which are prone to regular flooding, there are oak, fir and beech forests. Lime trees can also be found all over the country, and were once a feature of every village in Slovenia.

Many plants and some animal species are now in danger due to pollution, deforestation and the construction of settlements and roads. To prevent the situation from worsening some areas are now protected by law. Approximately 8 per cent of Slovenia has been designated national parks, regional parks or landscape parks.

▼ *The Slovene landscape is green with vegetation, including many types of forest.*

◀ The Triglav National Park covers an area of 838 square kilometres. Mount Triglav is situated almost in the middle of the park.

▼ Weasels are among the most common animals found in the region of the Triglav National Park.

Triglav National Park

As well as these parks there are 720 natural monuments, 34 national reserves and 77 natural monuments that are protected. The largest protected area is the Triglav National Park, which covers almost the entire Julian Alps. Within the park, natural places of interest such as glacial lakes, natural windows (naturally formed arches) and caves are protected. Special attention is paid to the protection of the vegetation, which includes the Triglav flower, Triglav gentian, edelweiss and several other plants. Some types of birds are also protected: the capercaillie, the black cock and the mountain eagle. Amongst the mammals
found in this region the best known are chamois (a type of antelope), ibex (a wild goat) and weasels.

Caves

The Škocjan caves in the south-west of Slovenia are known internationally, and scientists go there to study the limestone features. Škocjan has more than 5 km of underground passages, and caves that that are over 200 metres deep. They are registered on UNESCO's World Cultural and Natural Heritage List.

▶ The salt flats at Sečovlje are home to diverse
     ˪ are registered on the list of
          ˙rtant wetlands.

Animals

The vast and dense forests all over Slovenia offer protection to large mammals such as bears, lynxes and wolves. Of special interest are the animals that live in the watery underground areas. These creatures have adapted to living in permanent darkness. The best-known subterranean animal is the olm, a type of salamander that lives in underground freshwater lakes in the limestone landscapes of the Illyrian-Dinar region. The olm has become a symbol of Slovenian natural science.

▲ *Wild goats roam the high mountain slopes.*

Swamps play a significant role in the preservation of some amphibians. These swamps are also used as resting places by birds that migrate to warmer places in the autumn. The most important areas for migrating birds are the Sečovlje salt-pans, stagnant areas of the River Mura, the Cerknica Lake and the Ljubljana Marsh.

The symbol of the sub-Pannonian area of Slovenia (in the north-east) is the white stork, which likes to nest on chimney-tops and telegraph poles. In the River Soča the Soča trout is especially protected. The Karst sheepdog, which is a good sheep and cattle dog, and the Lipizzaner horse, are well known all across Europe. Both originated in Slovenia.

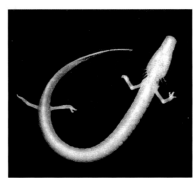

▲ *The cave salamander is common in Slovenia's karst (limestone) regions.*

◀ *The famous white stork is a declining species, which breeds in the warmer climates in Europe.*

The environment

Rapid development in transport infrastructures has led to an increase in environmental pollution, including noise and exhaust fumes. The construction of motorways is having a dramatic effect on the environment and interferes with and restricts the passage and movement of wild animals.

Today environmental issues are taken seriously in Slovenia. Young people are involved in various ecological movements. They contribute to a cleaner environment through such schemes as waste-paper collection, cleaning initiatives in their home environment, taking care of the natural environment, and playing a role in reforestation, all of which contribute to a greater ecological awareness.

▲ *The Lipizzaner horse evolved from Spanish, Italian and Arab stock that found its way to Slovenia. The horses are born dark brown or black, but turn white by the time they are eight years old.*

Environmental issues

Human activity can have a detrimental effect on the natural environment. One of the most serious of these is deforestation, when forests and woods are cut down. In towns the air is becoming polluted, and in some places the water is, too, as waste is dumped in rivers. Streams and groundwater are also in danger in some farming areas due to the overuse of artificial fertilisers, various chemical protective agents and machinery. In Slovenia great efforts are made to maintain a clean environment, although a number of rivers and groundwater systems have already been polluted. Despite this, the people are not always ecologically aware and do not recycle household waste, even though many towns provide special containers for this purpose. The construction of motorways is leading to a reduction in farmlands and forests.

Slovenia in the EU

Slovenia is a peaceful country and it welcomes visitors from all over the world. Its has a policy of peace towards all countries and has avoided the wars that have wreaked havoc in other former Yugoslav territories. It was accepted into the European Union on 1 May 2004.

After its declaration of independence in 1991, Slovenia started to build stronger links with Central and Western European countries. Slovenia is strengthening its international position and its reputation as a democratic, stable and successful European country. On 22 May 1992 it became a member of the United Nations. Slovenia contributes armed forces to UN peace operations and thus actively co-operates in preserving world peace.

Slovenia is also a member of the European Council, the World Trade Organization, the Central European Free Trade Agreement (CEFTA), the Organization for Security and Co-operation in Europe (OSCE) and a number of other international organisations. It also recently attained full membership of NATO and is campaigning for membership of the Organization for Economic Co-operation and Development (OECD). Amongst the basic goals of Slovenian foreign policy are stable, good neighbourly relations with Austria, Italy, Hungary and Croatia.

▲ *A Slovenian representative addresses the Global Congress on the issue of senior citizens.*

The Slovenian government tries its best to promote peace throughout the world. One of the key ways it does this is through the inter-national organisation UNICEF, which offers help to people all over the world who are suffering from poverty, hunger and disease.

◄ *US president George W. Bush and Slovenian prime minister Anton Rop during the ceremony to welcome new nations to NATO membership in March 2004.*

As a responsible member of the international community, Slovenia co-operates in political, military and civil endeavours to ensure security and stability in south-eastern Europe and further afield. It has also founded an international fund for de-mining (rendering land-mines harmless) and helping the victims of land-mines in Bosnia Herzegovina. These activities have already spread to the neighbouring Balkan countries.

The European Union

The Republic of Slovenia signed an agreement to join the European Union in 1996. The negotiations for becoming a full member started in March 1998 and were concluded in December 2002. The accession agreement was signed by Slovenia and nine other new member states in Athens on 16 April 2003.

After the signing, the agreement had to be ratified by all 15 existing members of the union and the European parliament, as well as by each of the 10 new member states. A referendum took place in Slovenia, during which citizens could vote about whether or not they wanted the country to become a member; 89.6 per cent of all Slovenes voted in favour of accession to the EU. In addition to the European parliament and the parliaments of the member states, the Slovene parliament will also ratify this agreement. The accession agreement became valid on 1 May 2004 and on this date Slovenia became a full member of the European Union.

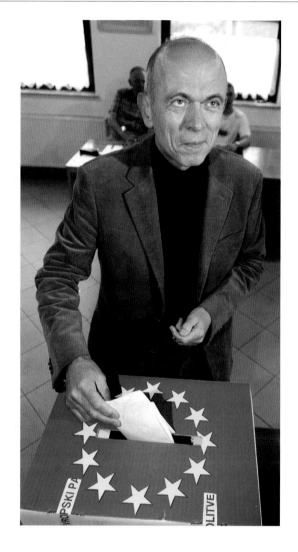

▲ The Slovenian president Janez Drnovsek casts his vote at a polling station in Ljubljana in June 2004, during the European elections.

◄ Slovenian children with scarfs showing the symbol of the European Union, celebrate their country becoming a member of the organisation in 2004.

Glossary

Celts A number of different tribes from central Europe, who had the same language and cultural roots.

Communism A policial system based on the principles of shared wealth and power.

Concentration camp Prison camps where Jews and other minority groups were sent by the Germans during the Second World War. Many died under the harsh conditions there.

Habsburg Empire The land under control of the German royal family, who gained the thrones of several countries, including Austria and Hungary, from the late Middle Ages to the twentieth century.

Orthodox Church The Christian Church in the East; it has several independent sects, including Greek Orthodox.

United Nations An organisation founded after the Second World War to promote peace and economic development in its member nations.

NATO North Atlantic Treaty Organization, established in 1949 to work towards security and co-operation between the member states.

Slavs A large group of European peoples with similar languages. Individual tribes descended from the Slavs, including Slovaks, Czechs, Poles, Serbs and Croats.

Index

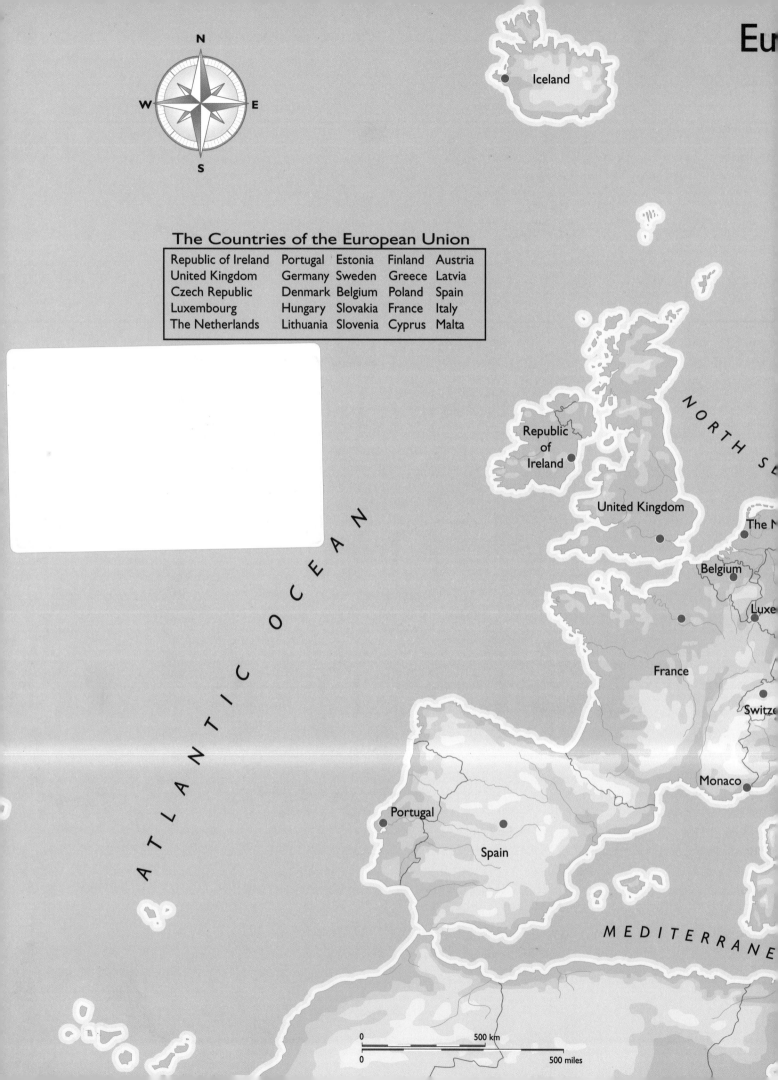

Eu

Iceland

The Countries of the European Union

Republic of Ireland	Portugal	Estonia	Finland	Austria
United Kingdom	Germany	Sweden	Greece	Latvia
Czech Republic	Denmark	Belgium	Poland	Spain
Luxembourg	Hungary	Slovakia	France	Italy
The Netherlands	Lithuania	Slovenia	Cyprus	Malta

N
W E
S

ATLANTIC OCEAN

NORTH SE

Republic of Ireland

United Kingdom

The N

Belgium

Luxe

France

Switze

Monaco

Portugal

Spain

MEDITERRANE

0   500 km

0   500 miles

Stencilling
made easy

Series Editors: Susan & Martin Penny

David & Charles

A DAVID & CHARLES BOOK

First published in the UK in 1998

A catalogue record for this book is available from the British Library.

ISBN 0 7153 0562 X

Series Editors: Susan & Martin Penny
Designed by Penny & Penny
Illustrations: Fred Fieber at Red Crayola
Photography: Ashton James; Jon Stone
Stylist: Susan Penny

Printed in France by Imprimerie Pollina S. A.
for David & Charles
Brunel House Newton Abbot Devon

Contents

✳ ✳ ✳ ✳ ✳ ✳ ✳

Introduction to Stencilling

Stencilling Made Easy is a complete guide to the craft of stencilling; we take you through the mysteries of which equipment to buy; give you hints on preparation, and the skills needed to cut stencils. By following the step-by-step instructions, you will quickly learn the essential techniques needed to create your own exciting projects

Making stencils

Below is a list of the essential equipment needed to cut stencils:

- **Stencil card** – thick yellow card, soaked in linseed oil to make it waterproof and pliable.
- **Acetate and stencil film** – a pliable clear plastic which can be drawn directly on to, and will show the design from below.
- **Cork** – pliable thin cork or a cork tile. Good for stencilling on fabric.
- **Paper** – use copier paper to trace or photocopy the design; useful when making masks for reverse stencilling.
- **Typewriter carbon paper** – use for transferring a tracing to stencil card.
- **Cutting mat** – a mat that self heals when cut and will protect your work surface.
- **Cutting knife** – slim, very sharp craft knife used for cutting stencil card or acetate.
- **Fine sandpaper** – use decorator's sandpaper for rubbing down wooden surfaces, and removing snags from the underside of stencils.

Painting with stencils

Below is a list of the essential equipment needed for painting stencil designs:

- **Stencil brush** – a stiff bristled brush with a flat top, made in different sizes and thicknesses.
- **Sponge** – use a natural sea sponge for a soft paint effect; or a synthetic sponge, cut from a kitchen scourer for a more textured effect.
- **Artist's paintbrush** – use to add highlights to a wet or dry stencilled design; or fine lines to flower stems or leaf veins.
- **Decorator's paintbrush** – use to apply a wash or base coat to wood; or to add a coat of varnish.
- **Dish for mixing paint** – use a plastic microwave dish, fresh food tray or tin foil dish; or a small artist's palette.
- **Kitchen paper** – useful for removing excess paint from a brush, mopping up spills and cleaning brushes.
- **Cotton buds** – used to clean stencils.
- **Cocktail stick** – used for mixing paint.

Tips for stencilling on tiles

- ✔ Use terracotta or unsealed floor tiles
- ✔ Seal the surface with matt emulsion paint
- ✔ Use acrylic paints on tiles, as they have the brightest colour range
- ✔ Apply the paint using a sponge
- ✔ Seal the stencilled tile with acrylic varnish
- ✔ Only use stencilled tiles in low wear areas

Tips for stencilling on wood

✔ Rub down the wood using fine sandpaper
✔ Colour the surface of bare wood with a wash
✔ Use spray adhesive to mount the stencil
✔ Seal the stencilled wood with acrylic varnish

Tips for stencilling on metal

✔ Rub down with wet and dry sandpaper
✔ Use a spray primer to seal the bare metal
✔ Allow to dry before removing the stencil
✔ Seal the surface with polyurethane varnish

Tips for stencilling on paper

✔ Use uncoated paper
✔ Do not overload the paper with paint
✔ Spray paint will give the best finish
✔ Doilies make good masks for stencilling
✔ Leave the stencilled paper to dry flat

Tips for stencilling on fabric

✔ Use calico or cotton based fabric
✔ Wash to remove 'finishing' and shrinkage
✔ Test the paint on the fabric, for bleeding
✔ Fix fabric paint with an iron before washing
✔ Use fabric paint for most fabrics; emulsion paint can be used on stiff fabric like hessian
✔ Seal emulsion with a PVA glue/water mix

Choosing the right paint

Choosing the right paint for the right surface can be difficult: listed below are some of the plus and minus points to help you make that choice.

● **Stencil paint** – Water-based
  The right consistency for stencilling
  Colours can be mixed
  Will give good results on most surfaces
  Brushes can be washed in water
  Use water-based varnish to seal
  Very expensive compared with acrylics

● **Acrylic** – Water-based
  The right consistency for stencilling
  Colours can be mixed
  Large range of colours available
  Will give good results on most surfaces
  Brushes can be washed in water
  Dries fast, may need a 'retarder'
  Use water-based varnish to seal

● **Emulsion** – Water-based
  Sold in small tester pots
  Mostly pale colours, but can be mixed
  Too slow to dry for most projects
  Paint thin, but works well on fabric

● **Fabric paint** – Water-based
  Some makes too thin for stencilling
  Colours can be mixed
  Test for 'bleeding'
  Brushes can be washed in water
  Iron fix before laundering

● **Enamel paint** – Oil-based
  Use on metal surfaces
  Brushes must be cleaned in white spirit
  Work in a well ventilated room

● **Spray paint** – Most are cellulose based
  Must be stored at room temperature
  Use in a well ventilated room
  Shake well, spray from 30-46cm (12-18in)

● **Matt acrylic varnish** – Water-based
  Brush and spray-on
  Wash brushes in water
  No smell and dries very quickly

● **Polyurethane varnish** – Oil-based
  Brush-on, very slow to dry
  Wash brushes in white spirit
  Work in a well ventilated room

Making Stencils

A stencil can be cut from almost any flat material: card, acetate, clear film, cork or paper. How you make a stencil and what you make it from depends on the craft materials that are available to you. The recommended method of working is given within each project, but you may prefer to try a different technique

Using carbon paper

To transfer the design to stencil card, place typewriter carbon paper between the card and the tracing. Draw over the lines firmly using a ball-point pen.

Cutting a stencil

Hold the uncut stencil on a cutting mat and following the design lines, start cutting from the centre. Move the stencil as you cut, drawing the knife towards you.

Using acetate

To transfer the design to clear acetate or stencil film, place a tracing of the design under the acetate or film then draw over the lines firmly using a felt-tipped pen.

Rubbing down

After cutting the stencil, check the underside for snags – these should be removed using fine sandpaper, to ensure the stencil will fit snugly when attached to the prepared surface.

Mounting a stencil

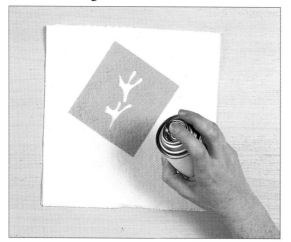

Lay the stencil face down on paper. Working in a well ventilated room, coat the back with spray mount adhesive – this will keep the stencil flat while painting, but can easily be removed with white spirit. Position the stencil on the prepared painting surface, holding in place with masking tape.

Repairing a stencil

To repair a stencil if you make a mistake whilst cutting or it gets broken while in use: clean around the area to be mended, then lay the stencil on a cutting mat covering the break with sticky tape. Turn the stencil over and repeat on the other side. Cut away the excess tape using a sharp craft knife.

Making a leaf stencil

To make a stencil from a leaf or flat object: attach the leaf or object to a thin cork sheet using sticky tape. Draw around the shape with a felt-tipped pen. Place the cork on a cutting mat and, using a sharp craft knife or small scissors, cut around the drawn shape, neatening any points or corners.

Using a cookie cutter

To scribble stencil on to fabric: position a cookie cutter on to the prepared fabric, holding firmly with one hand. Using a fabric painting felt pen and starting at the top, scribble from side to side within the cutter, touching each side as you move down towards the bottom of the shape.

Painting Techniques

Traditionally stencil paint is applied using a flat-ended brush, but you may want to try another method of applying the paint. A sponge dipped in paint and dabbed on to the surface will give a mottled folk art look; or you could try using spray paint to give a finer, more even paint finish

Loading the brush

Load the stencil brush with paint, then dab on to kitchen paper to remove the excess paint, giving an almost dry brush. Do this each time you add paint to the brush.

Adding highlights

To highlight the design: using a small stencil brush, dab paint on to the wet or dry stencilled design, at the edges or the centre to give a three-dimensional effect.

Pouncing

Using a loaded stencil brush, apply paint to the parts of the design not covered by the stencil. Use a soft pouncing or gentle circular movement with the brush.

Sponging

Dip a piece of sponge into the paint. Dab the sponge on to the design area not covered by the stencil. Apply the paint lightly to create a mottled effect.

Using a doily

In a well ventilated room, lightly coat the back of a doily with spray mount adhesive, then position right side up on a sheet of paper. Shake the paint can, then holding upright, spray the doily and the paper between, from a distance of 30-46cm (12-18in). Remove the doily, leave to dry.

Reverse stencilling

Stretch the material on to card, then mask off the areas not to be painted: use paper shapes attached with tape or torn masking tape strips. Using a large stencil brush, dab fabric paint on to the material, building up the colour slowly. Leave to dry, then remove the paper shapes. To fix the paint, see page 12.

Cleaning a stencil

Keep the stencil free from paint by cleaning both sides between applications. Use kitchen paper and a cotton bud dipped in water to remove water based paint; for oil based paint use white spirit. Good adhesion to the surface will stop the paint 'bleeding' behind the stencil.

Washing brushes

Wash brushes in warm soapy water at regular intervals while in use, and when changing paint colour – this will stop a build-up of paint. Clean and dry the brushes thoroughly before storing upright. A rubber band wrapped around the bristles will help keep them in good condition.

Painting on Fabric

Stencilling on fabric requires extra care in preparation and finishing: fabric should be washed to remove the 'finishing', then ironed on a fluffy towel. For fabric that cannot be laundered, coat with a mix of PVA glue and water. This will seal the surface, protecting it from dirt

Preparing fabric

Fabric should be laundered before applying paint to remove the 'finishing' and take-up any shrinkage in the fabric: wash in warm soapy water, then iron on a fluffy towel.

Fixing fabric paint

Stencilled fabric should be heat fixed to stop the paint washing out. Place the dry fabric face down on a towel. Iron for 1-2 minutes on the hottest setting suitable for the fabric.

Using fabric paint

Working with an almost dry brush, pounce paint within the design area of the stencil. Remove the stencil, clean, then reposition on the fabric. To fix the paint, see above.

Sealing surfaces

To protect fabric that is difficult to launder: coat with PVA glue mixed with an equal quantity of water, working the mix into the weave of the fabric. Dry flat for several days.

Preparing the window box

1 Smooth down any rough surfaces on your window box with sandpaper before applying one coat of wood primer. Allow to dry.

2 Using emulsion, paint two coats on the front, back and sides of the window box. Pick out any decorative features such as a scalloped top in yellow.

Positioning the stencil

1 Lay the stencil face down on a piece of newspaper. Finely coat the back of the stencil with spray mount adhesive: the adhesive will hold the stencil firmly while painting the design, but can easily be removed with a little white spirit.

2 Position the stencil on the project, holding firmly in place with small pieces of masking tape. To position the stencil on the window box, use a ruler and chalk; if your box is wider than the project example, you may be able to fit three or more repeat patterns along the front and back. In which case, position and paint the central design first, then re-position the stencil working outwards.

3 When positioning the second stencil make sure that it is the same height and distance from the sides and the top. The project example shows both roses and daisies stencils also being used in reverse. If you wish to do this clean and dry the stencil before turning it over.

Painting the window box

1 Using a stencil brush apply paint in a soft pouncing, circular movement to the flowers and the leaves. Use a clean brush for each colour and do not overload with paint. The roses are painted white, yellow and red with yellow detail and green leaves; the daisies are white with yellow and blue detail. When dry

apply highlights in toning colours. Allow to dry completely before removing the stencil.

2 If any bleeding has occurred on to the background, touch-up with a fine brush using the appropriate background colour.

Painting the flower pot

1 Paint the outside of the flower pot with a coat of wood primer, to seal the porous surface of the pot; leave to dry. Paint the outside of the pot with a coat of red emulsion paint and the rim yellow.

2 Position the daisy stencil on to the front of the pot, and hold in place with small pieces of masking tape. Apply paint to the design using the same colours as the window box. Allow to dry before removing the stencil.

Painting the watering can

1 If you are using an old metal watering can, smooth down any rough surfaces using wet and dry sandpaper.

2 Wipe over the surface with a damp cloth to remove any dust, then apply one coat of metal primer to the outside of the can. Allow to dry.